Little Voices
Film Music

My Favorite Things
(from 'The Sound Of Music') 2

Over The Rainbow
(from 'The Wizard Of Oz') 8

Pure Imagination
(from 'Willy Wonka & The Chocolate Factory') 14

Singin' In The Rain
(from 'Singin' In The Rain') 19

Truly Scrumptious
(from 'Chitty Chitty Bang Bang') 26

Published by
Novello Publishing Limited
14-15 Berners Street, London, W1T 3LJ, UK.

Exclusive Distributors:
Hal Leonard
7777 West Bluemound Road
Milwaukee, WI 53213
Email: info@halleonard.com
Hal Leonard Europe Limited
42 Wigmore Street
Marylebone, London, W1U 2RN
Email: info@halleonardeurope.com
Hal Leonard Australia Pty. Ltd.
4 Lentara Court
Cheltenham, Victoria, 3192 Australia
Email: info@halleonard.com.au

Order No. NOV163647   ISBN 978-1-78305-106-9
This book © Copyright 2013 Novello & Company Limited.

Arranged by Barrie Carson Turner.
Edited by Ruth Power.
Music processed by Paul Ewers Music Design.

Piano by Paul Knight.
Singers: Rachel Lindley, Sinead O'Kelly, Lucy Potterton.
Engineered, mixed & mastered by Jonas Persson.

Printed in the EU.

NOVELLO PUBLISHING LIMITED

CW00504488

My Favorite Things
(from 'The Sound Of Music')

Words by Oscar Hammerstein
Music by Richard Rodgers

ket - tles and warm wool - en mit - tens, brown pa - per pack - ag - es
sleigh - bells and schnitz - el with noo - dles, wild geese that fly with the

ket - tles, warm wool - en mit - tens, brown pa - per pack - ag - es
sleigh - bells, schnitz - el with noo - dles, wild geese that fly with the

Cm⁷   F⁷

tied up with string; these are a few of my fa - vor - ite
moon on their wings; these are a few of my fa - vor - ite

tied up with string are a few of my fa - vor - ite
moon on their wings are a few of my fa - vor - ite

B♭/D   E♭/G   B♭/F   E♭   Am⁷⁽♭5⁾

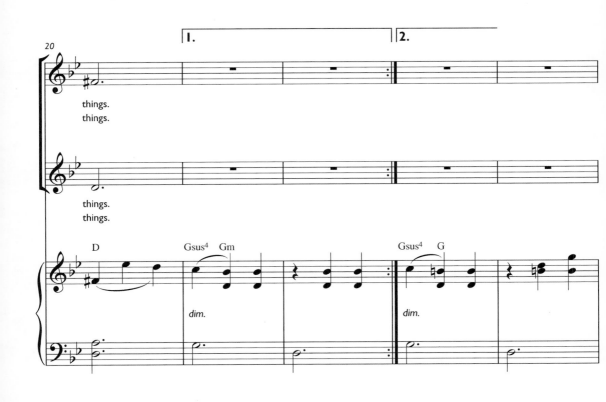

things.
things.

things.
things.

1.

2.

D   Gsus⁴ Gm   Gsus⁴ G

dim.   dim.

mf

Girls in white dress - es with blue sat - in sash - es, snow - flakes that

mf

Girls in white dress - es, sat - in sash - es, snow - flakes,

mf

C⁷

When the dog bites, when the bee stings, when I'm feel - ing

When the dog bites, when the bee stings, when I'm feel - ing

sad,_____ I sim - ply re - mem - ber my fa - vor - ite things and

sad,_____ I sim - ply re - mem - ber my fa - vor - ite things and

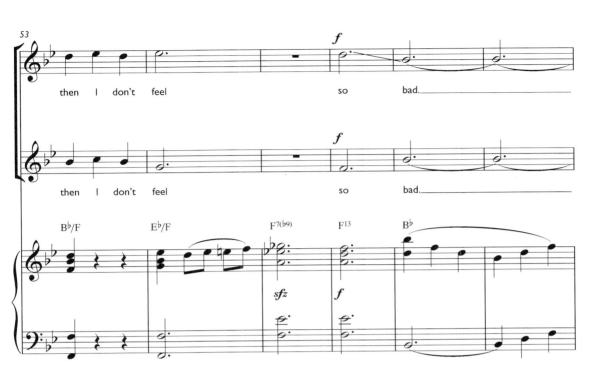

then I don't feel so bad.

then I don't feel so bad.

Over The Rainbow
(from 'The Wizard Of Oz')

Words by E.Y. Harburg
Music by Harold Arlen

9

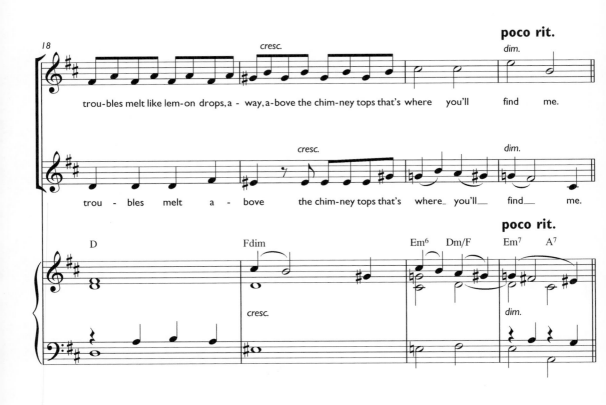

trou-bles melt like lem-on drops, a - way, a-bove the chim-ney tops that's where you'll find me.

trou - bles melt a - bove the chim-ney tops that's where you'll find me.

Some - where o - ver the rain - bow, blue - birds fly.

Some - where o - ver the rain - bow, blue - birds fly.

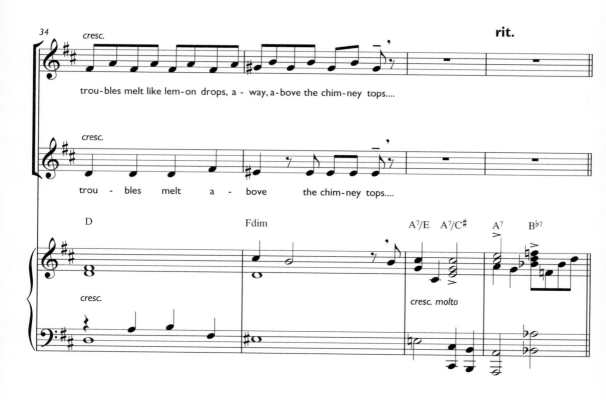

Pure Imagination
(from 'Willy Wonka & The Chocolate Factory')

Words & Music by
Leslie Bricusse & Anthony Newley

look and you'll see   your im - ag - i - na - tion. We'll be -

look and you'll see in - to your im - ag - i - na - tion. We'll be -

-gin with a spin. Trav - 'ling in the world of my cre -

-gin with a spin. Trav - 'ling in the world of my cre -

15

-a - tion. What we'll see will de - fy ex - pla - na - tion.

-a - tion. What we'll see will de - fy ex - pla - na - tion.

F#m7   Bm7   Em7   A9   F#9

If you want to view Pa - ra - dise, sim - ply look a - round and view it.

If you want to view Pa - ra - dise, sim - ply look a - round, and

Gmaj7   F#m   Em9   Dmaj7

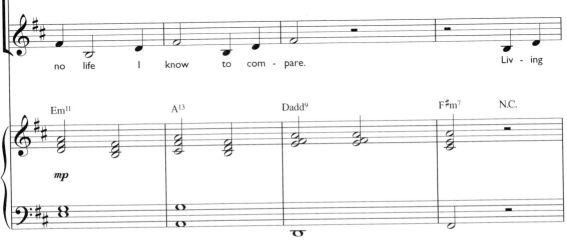

there you'll be free if you tru - ly wish to be. Come with

there you'll be free if you tru - ly wish to be. Come with

Em⁷ A¹³ Dmaj⁷ A⁷ D N.C.

2.
rit.

tru - ly wish to be._____

tru - ly wish to be._____

rit.

F♯maj⁷ F⁷/A A⁷ N.C. D

Singin' In The Rain
(from 'Singin' In The Rain')

Words by Arthur Freed
Music by Nacio Herb Brown

sun's___ in my heart___ and I'm rea - dy for love. Let the

the sun's in my heart I'm rea - dy for, for love.___

storm - y clouds chase ev - 'ry - one___ from the place, come

Let the storm-y clouds chase___ ev - 'ry - one from the place,___

on_____ with the rain, I've a smile_____ on my face. I'll

come on with the rain, I've a smile_____ on my face.

F#dim⁷   C⁷   Gm⁷   C⁷

walk   down   the   lane   with a   hap - py re - frain,   and

Walk down   the   lane   with a   hap-py re - frain,   and

Gm   C⁷   Gm   C⁷

Fine

sing - in',_____ just sing - in' in_____ the rain._____

sing - in', I'm just sing - in' in_____ the rain._____

F   C⁷   F

1. Why am I smil - in' and why do I sing?____ Why does De -
2. Why do they call me the boy with the smile?____ When did I

1. Why am I smil - in' and why do I sing,____ why do I sing?
2. Why do they call me the boy with the smile,____ boy with the smile?

D♭⁷   F⁶   D♭⁷

mf

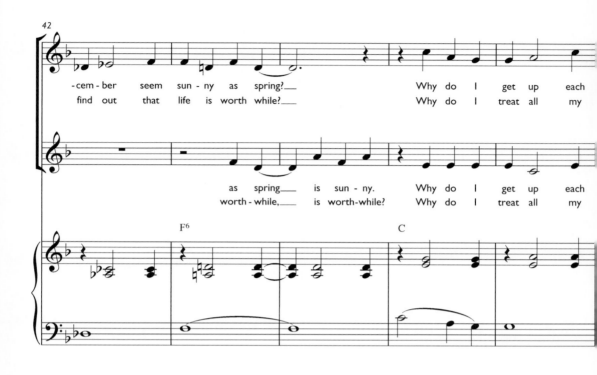

-cem - ber seem sun - ny as spring?___ Why do I get up each
find out that life is worth while?___ Why do I treat all my

as spring___ is sun - ny. Why do I get up each
worth - while,___ is worth-while? Why do I treat all my

F⁶   C

morn - ing to start___ hap - py and het up, with joy in my heart?_
trou - bles with scorn?___ See - ing the rain - bow be - fore it is born._

morn - ing___ hap - py and het up, with joy___
troub - les? See - ing the rain - bow be - fore___

F   D   G⁷

Why is each new task a tri-fle to do?____ Be-
Why am I sure all my dreams will come true?____ Be-

____ in my heart?____ a tri-fle to do?____
____ it is born.____ my dreams will come true?____

A♭7   D♭

1.   2.   *D.S. al Fine*
                                    mf

- cause I am liv-ing a life full of you.____ I'm
- cause I am bank-ing my whole world on you.____ I'm
                                    I'm
                                    ____ *mf*

a life full of you.____ I'm
my whole world on you.____ I'm

E♭♭9   D♭7   C7   C7

Truly Scrumptious
(from 'Chitty Chitty Bang Bang')

Words & Music by
Richard M. Sherman & Robert B. Sherman

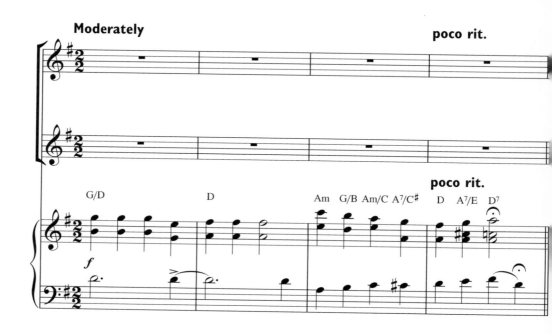

Toot sweets sound like what they are. So do lol - lies in a lol - li - pop jar.

Gin-ger-bread men have a gin-ger-bread sound, we've found.

Gin-ger-bread men have a gin-ger-bread sound, we've found.

Am   G/B Am/C A⁷/C♯   D   D⁷   G   Am⁷/D   D⁷

Sug-ar plum, cin-na-mon and lem-on tart   tell you what they are right from the start. And

Sug-ar plum, cin-na-mon and lem-on tart___   tell you what they are right from the start. And

G   D⁷   B⁷   Em

cresc.

rit.

dim.

your name_____ does the same for you,_____ by co - in - ci- dence:

dim.

your_____ name does the same for you, by co - in - ci- dence:

G/A   A⁷   D⁷

dim.

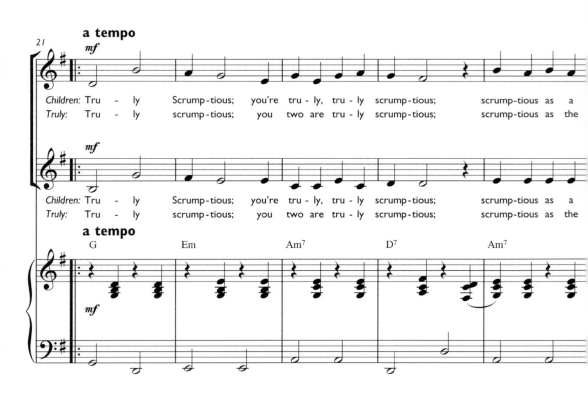

a tempo

mf

Children: Tru - ly Scrump-tious; you're tru - ly, tru - ly scrump-tious; scrump-tious as a
Truly: Tru - ly scrump-tious; you two are tru - ly scrump-tious; scrump-tious as the

mf

Children: Tru - ly Scrump-tious; you're tru - ly, tru - ly scrump-tious; scrump-tious as a
Truly: Tru - ly scrump-tious; you two are tru - ly scrump-tious; scrump-tious as the

a tempo

G   Em   Am⁷   D⁷   Am⁷

mf

to our wish - es. Tru - ly Scrump-tious, though we may seem pre - sump - tuous,
to my wish - es. Tru - ly scrump-tious, you two are tru - ly scrump-tious,

nev - er, nev - er ev - er go a - way._____
and I shan't for - get this love - ly day._____

nev - er, nev - er ev - er go a - way, don't go a - way.
and I shan't for - get this love - ly day, this love - ly day.

Track Listing

1. My Favorite Things
(from 'The Sound Of Music')
(Hammerstein/Rodgers)
Imagem Music
Full Performance

2. Over The Rainbow
(from 'The Wizard Of Oz')
(Harburg/Arlen)
EMI United Partnership Limited
Full Performance

3. Pure Imagination
(from 'Willy Wonka & The Chocolate Factory')
(Bricusse/Newley)
Imagem Songs Limited
Full Performance

4. Singin' In The Rain
(from 'Singin' In The Rain')
(Freed/Brown)
EMI United Partnership Limited
Full Performance

5. Truly Scrumptious
(from 'Chitty Chitty Bang Bang')
(Sherman/Sherman)
EMI United Partnership Limited
Full Performance

6. My Favorite Things
(from 'The Sound Of Music')
(Hammerstein/Rodgers)
Imagem Music
Piano Accompaniment

7. Over The Rainbow
(from 'The Wizard Of Oz')
(Harburg/Arlen)
EMI United Partnership Limited
Piano Accompaniment

8. Pure Imagination
(from 'Willy Wonka & The Chocolate Factory')
(Bricusse/Newley)
Imagem Songs Limited
Piano Accompaniment

9. Singin' In The Rain
(from 'Singin' In The Rain')
(Freed/Brown)
EMI United Partnership Limited
Piano Accompaniment

10. Truly Scrumptious
(from 'Chitty Chitty Bang Bang')
(Sherman/Sherman)
EMI United Partnership Limited
Piano Accompaniment